IF LOVE IS CONTAGIOUS, I HOPE YOU NEVER GET WELL!

Janie Jasin

"No Limits" Publishing
1743 Green Crest Dr.
Victoria MN 55386-9400
ph 952-443-3086   fx 952-443-3081

www.janiespeaks.con

If Love Is Contagious, I Hope You Never Get Well!
By Janie Jasin

Copyright© 1984 Janie Jasin

Cover design: Terry Dugan
Editor: Jodie Ahern

10 9 8 7 6 5 4

ISBN 0-916773-01-9

Printed in the United States of America

This book is dedicated to YOU if you ever:

- ...wondered what you were going to be when you grew up

- ...felt hopelessly inadequate and unmotivated in college, high school, or trade school

- ...went to sleep hoping you'd wake up thin

- ...felt lost in a daze of chemicals and cried alone in a darkened room

- ...got tired and didn't know what else to do to help your child grow up to have a meaningful life

or muttered the words, "God grant me the serenity to accept the things I cannot change, the courage to change the things I can, and the wisdom to know the difference."

I also dedicate this book to every counselor who loved enough to be tough, and to

> Mom and Daddy
> to Jeff, Janet, and Joe
> and to Frankie Finch, my most affirming friend, who has made life blessed and good and valuable.

TABLE OF CONTENTS

Essays

    I. Uncle Carlton 1

    II. Sheaves of Wheat 6

    III. Mr. Beecher 10

    IV. Rosemary 15

    V. Enough 18

    VI. Shelly 21

    VII. Beige 25

    VIII. Matthew 29

    IX. Stuff 34

    X. Change 38

    XI. Blooming Prairie, MN 55917 42

    XII. Flags 47

Short Pieces

    I. Success Is 53

    II. Alone For Awhile 54

    III. Higher Power 57

    IV. She Was Twenty-One Yesterday 58

    V. The Separation 61

    VI. Brief-Case Barbie 63

    VII. True Identity 65

If Love Is Contagious, I Hope You Never Get Well

I had to learn how to love, and for me the learning was long and hard. My life didn't really begin until I learned how to love, to be loved, and to love myself. I went through my own hell first, some of it my own making, some of it perhaps by happenstance. But Lord, have I learned.

After ten years of marriage, three children, and a house most people would envy, I got into trouble. The trouble was that I lost touch with other people and, at the same time, I lost touch with myself.

At first, the trouble was alcoholism. And then the trouble was loneliness. And then it was obsessive eating. And then it was drugs. I would trade one destructive compulsion for another.

I learned, in my recovery, that PEOPLE NEED OTHER PEOPLE. We are all on one long pilgrimage together, and we need to give and get as much help along the way as we can.

The stories in this book are about the people I've met along the way. I've learned through them to relate the love, the wonderment, and the discovery of the innermost goodness that comes from the affirmation of each of us as human beings.

This affirmation is now my guiding force. It gives meaning and purpose and direction to my life. I don't feel lost anymore. I may not always know where I'm going, but I always seem to get there!

J.J.

Essays

UNCLE CARLTON

At my Uncle Carlton's funeral a few years ago, there was a noticeable lack of your basic "wailing and gnashing of teeth." As a matter of fact, I heard quite a few gentle chuckles coming from small clusters of relatives as they exchanged memories of this cherished man. I, too, found myself smiling as I played back my own mental slide show of Uncle Carlton.

It's not that we didn't grieve at Uncle Carlton's passing. We wept as much as we laughed. But I think Uncle Carlton would have wanted us to celebrate his move from one existence to another. I imagined him celebrating the event himself up in heaven, with all his new pals, Saint Peter and the gang—particularly Saint Francis, who would have made certain that all Uncle Carlton's dearly departed dogs were waiting for him. Jiggers and Smokey and Missy, wagging their little angel-dog tails.

OK, maybe I did get a little carried away. But the point is that Uncle Carlton was a truly loving, joyous soul and he managed to impart his particular brand of simple joy to just about everyone he touched, including me, his niece and godchild. Without ever becoming preachy or philosophical, Uncle Carlton showed me by his simple daily actions what it means to love life and all that it brings.

He made me feel very special. Uncle Carlton had other nieces and nephews and godchildren, but when I was with him, I felt like the one and only. I know the others felt that way, too. Many of them said so later.

When I was little, Uncle Carlton would take me by the hand and march me into the dime store, announcing to all who would listen, "This is Janie, my niece from Milwaukee." Somehow, being from Milwaukee made me singularly important. Then Uncle Carlton would buy me a coloring book and later we would color it together. He really *talked* to me, too. Not in the usual nice-little-cutie-pie voice that adults so often adopt with children, but in a real conversational tone, sometimes serious, sometimes funny, but always respectful.

He showed me the joy in little things: tartar sauce on rye bread, pecan puffs from the local drugstore, ice cream on hot summer nights, and, above all, the friendship of a dog. He loved his dogs. I remember a black curly dog and a smooth-haired dog, and two beagles, who grew fat from all the treats Uncle Carlton smuggled to them from my aunt's kitchen.

We'd all pile into the car—the dogs, Uncle Carlton, Aunt Jennie, and me—and go for wonderful breezy rides, the dogs lolling their tongues out the window, and Uncle Carlton pointing out things to me that I would never have noticed on my own.

Uncle Carlton was a religious man, but never an oppressive Bible-thumper. He would sit me on his lap during quiet times and read little verses from the backs of holy cards while I examined the paintings of angels and saints. The dogs would all sit around our feet, gnawing their bones and looking up occasionally at some inflection in my uncle's voice. I thought the dogs were praying, too. I called their bones "prayer bones," imagining the dogs were conducting some spiritual ritual of their own.

Uncle Carlton shared his simple religious beliefs with his wife. When I recall their happiness together, I understand that it was not a matter of their particular brand of religion, it was just love. They loved each other and they loved all of us, and we were all *affirmed* by their love. It was that simple.

But there was a time in my life when I shunned my Uncle Carlton's simple ways. Oh, he was *too* simple, I thought, when I was seventeen. I was much too big to sit on his lap, much too sophisticated to eat tartar sauce on rye bread. The dogs got hairs all over my skirt-and-sweater sets, and I no longer believed in the verses on the backs of Uncle Carlton's holy cards. When I abandoned my childish ways, I abandoned Uncle Carlton along with them. Suddenly I was far too busy to visit him. There were more important things to do.

There were parties and dates, there were dances and college. And later, there was marriage and there were children, a home on the lake, furniture and boats. . . and, all the while, there was a terrible emptiness that I tried frantically to fill.

When finally there were no more diversions left to occupy me, I remembered my Uncle Carlton's simple ways. I had never felt empty or lonely with him. And it had not taken very much to make us happy. Only gentle companionship and loving laughter. It really *had* been that simple.

It wasn't too late. I went back to visit my Uncle Carlton, and he was there, waiting patiently for his "niece from Milwaukee." It was as if I had never left. The pain of my emptiness subsided, and I felt whole again. AFFIRMED.

Uncle Carlton and I saw a lot more of each other after that. We talked shortly before his death. I felt privileged to have been his godchild.

And so at his funeral, it seemed right to celebrate his life as well as to mourn his death. He had left something behind in every one of us. He would live on.

I have this great vision of another celebration—of me and Uncle Carlton reunited in heaven, the heaven of his holy cards. The dogs will be there, Jiggers and Smokey and Missy. The banquet table will be laid with tartar sauce on rye bread, pecan puffs from the old drugstore, candy from Oakes' general store, and Uncle Carlton's favorite West End fish. Everybody will be laughing. All the things Uncle Carlton believed in will have come true. And he will take me by the hand and lead me around, saying, "Jesus, Saint Peter, Saint Francis—I would like you all to welcome Janie, my niece from Milwaukee."

SHEAVES OF WHEAT

When dancing the mazurka with an immense hog farmer clad in heavy-duty denim moved me to tears of sincere patriotism, I knew I had reached a new level of...well, of something.

It happened in the early days of my public-speaking career, when my dear friend Frankie Finch used to provide piano music as an accompaniment to whatever it was I was doing. Actually, I'm not sure even today what I *was* doing, but it felt right, and the music tied it all together and made it fun.

Frankie had been a dancer, and she had a musical response to almost everything. If someone in the audience introduced herself as "Mary," right away Frankie would burst into the opening line of "Mary Is a Grand Old Name." Or someone else might mention that he was on the company softball team and Frankie would be right there with "Take Me Out to the Ballgame."

After a workshop at the agricultural school in rural Canby, Minnesota, Frankie and I were feeling particularly pleased with ourselves. They liked us! I mean they REALLY liked us! So much so that one of the organizers of the talk came up to us after our presentation and said, "Say, Janie, we're thinking that maybe we'd like you to come back here and talk to some of the producers out here. (Producers, we learned, means farmers, not movie moguls.) You see, the crops have been kind of bad, and morale is low..."

The man knew just how to get me. Boosting sagging morale had become my life's work. I agreed to do the workshop. Only then did I think to ask just who these "producers" were.

"Oh, well, there's Mr. So-and-So, he raises hogs, and then there's Mr. Whatshisname, he raises hogs, too, and there's that hog farmer, you know..." There seemed to be a recurring theme.

I may be a city kid, but I was game. But then again, who was I to barge in there and tell those hog farmers how to get it together? I had to do some serious research first. So I said to the director, "I don't know too much about pigs. I think we should go out to the farm and see them firsthand. If we are going to make up four hours about pigs and wheat and stuff, I gotta FEEL it!"

Frankie kicked me, but I pretended not to notice.

The men were delighted to take us out to their farms and show us around. Frankie clung to my purse, terrified of the huge animals. They really were big, too. There we were, mincing around in our Pappagallos among these giant porkers as they snorted and grunted and did vaguely repulsive pig-type things.

But I really began to get a feel for the life these farmers led. They were very warm and friendly, and later they took us into their homes and fed us homemade cakes and showed us pictures of their daughters and talked about their strong ties to and feelings about their land.

After the farm visits, Frankie and I got together to plan the workshop. What would we do? I had been inspired by the significance of the land, so I decided that's what we'd talk about—The Land! Frankie began to hum, "This Land Is Your Land..." Sure! Then she began to fill in her own words, using the rural Canby lingo we had picked up. But how were we going to get the farmers involved?

Suddenly I had a vision. "I can see it now," I whispered, thinking of a great Busby Berkeley-type number, with a chorus line of farmers waving sheaves of wheat. Frankie would lead the singing and dancing, dressed in denim, of course. But how could she play the piano if she was flitting around the room like Lady Bountiful, scattering seeds?

"I'll tape some organ music!" she decided.

So we got together to make the recording, and as we sang the words and played the song, we both began to cry at the thought of our great country and its land and its devoted tenders and tillers of the soil. It moved us. We really got *into* it!

I have to admit, though, that after we made the recording, we felt pretty silly. I mean, there we were, dancing and singing and crying all at the same time, over "This Land..."

After the music was taken care of, we still had one problem—the wheat sheaves. Everyone would have one, we had decided. But just what WAS a wheat sheaf, anyway? One stalk, or a group of them? How many? How long? How many wheat sheaves make one amber wave of grain? Back to the research.

Eventually we made the sheaves. We used cardboard and fabric and construction paper and glue. If I made one, I must have made 110 of them.

That night at the Tower Motel in Canby, Minnesota, we did it all. We danced and sang and waved our wheat sheaves. And the farmers told us about their lives, about what it's like when the crop is bad. Frankie and I were allowed a look into these farmers' hearts and minds. We were totally immersed in their lives, and there really was a simple elemental purity to them. It was a wonderful night.

And that's why grand thoughts of history and patriotism and love and work that came to mind when I danced the mazurka with Mr. So-and-So brought tears to my eyes. Also to his, I think.

MR. BEECHER

When I was first married, I worked as a social director at a beautiful nursing home. Can't you just picture me: a youthful Florence Nightingale dressed in my summer frock and white gloves, gingerly emptying bedpans instead of executing my grand plans for social activities and movies and good times for the patients?

I had chosen to work at one of the least threatening facilities I could find—the Sleepy Hollow Manor Nursing Home in Falls Church, Virginia, a new and quite elegant residence. The very name of the place had a sedative effect, and I hoped to just tiptoe around doing good works without getting too involved in anything "unpleasant."

But I did get involved. There weren't too many patients there, so it was easy to get acquainted with each one. It was very enlightening for me as a young woman to learn the life stories of some of those old people, and to see how they lived. There is a richness to their lives that we so often overlook, a quality that we will understand only when we, too, are old.

One day, an old man was brought in by the attendants. He seemed totally spent, absolutely helpless. His family stood around as he was settled into his room. I was interested in all this, and I asked one of the nurses about him.

She said, "Oh, that's Mr. Beecher. He hasn't fed himself for over six months. He hasn't even been able to sit up for over three months. He hasn't walked for over a year." She smiled sadly and shook her head; she had seen such patients before. Patients who were not ill, but who had simply given up.

I approached the family and asked if there was anything I could do to help Mr. Beecher. They told me, "Don't bother too much. There's not much left of him."

"But that just can't be!" I thought. He couldn't just give up!

I began to visit Mr. Beecher daily. I'd bounce into his room each day and say, quite gaily, "Hello, Mr. Beecher!"

Nothing.

"How are you, today, Mr. Beecher?"

Nothing.

Everyone thought I was wasting my time, but I kept up my daily visits. Once he did answer me. He said, "G-r-r-r-r." I took it as a positive sign.

Not too long after Mr. Beecher arrived, a woman named Harriet was brought in. Harriet was a sketch, she really was. She was spirited and lively, and she took great pains with her appearance. Each day, she coiffed her grey-blue hair into an elaborate "do" and pinned a large, gaudy brooch to her bright paisley dress. She smoked, waving her cigarette about in emphatic gestures, unconscious of the ashes that dropped all over her, leaving enough tiny, circular burns in her dresses to give them the appearance of Swiss cheese. Harriet was really a character, and everyone loved her.

She was so charming, in fact, that I thought to myself, if anyone can make Mr. Beecher come out of his shell, Harriet can. I asked her, "Harriet, would you go in to see Mr. Beecher? See what you can find out about him?"

"Sure," Harriet said obligingly, and winked a mascara-rimmed eye confidently.

That afternoon, Harriet found me in the cafeteria and drew up a chair to report her findings. She seemed to be enjoying her role as undercover investigator. She told me in a stage whisper, "Mr. Beecher was one of the top architects in Washington, D.C., in his day. In fact, he designed one of the archives buildings there for the *government*!"

I was dumbfounded. Not by the information, but by the fact that Harriet had actually gotten Mr. Beecher to talk. Obviously, his work must be very important to him. I decided right then to follow up on

Harriet's lead, and to use that subject to open Mr. Beecher up to the rest of the world.

Shortly after Harriet had done her espionage, I happened to be in Washington. I found the building she had told me about, and it was true! Mr. Beecher had designed it! Somehow I was able to obtain a copy of Mr. Beecher's original blueprint from the basement files of the building, and I returned to the nursing home with eager anticipation.

Clutching the rolled-up document, I breezed into Mr. Beecher's room. "Hello, Mr. Beecher!"

Nothing.

Then I scolded, "Mr. Beecher, you have really been holding out on us." His eyes widened. I unrolled the blueprint and held it before him. "Did you design this building?" I demanded.

Mr. Beecher sat up in his bed and his mouth started trembling, and he said, "Yes, I did. Would you like me to tell you about it?"

I sat down, and he began to talk about his work. He said he didn't think that anyone was really interested in architecture until "that lovely Harriet" came in to inquire. In fact, Mr. Beecher talked more about Harriet than he did about architecture. Eventually, Harriet came in to talk with us. The room was absolutely charged with emotion coming from those two people—old folks with "not much left" to live for.

Harriet and Mr. Beecher got married that year. He was 89 and she was 92. I'm not sure Harriet ever realized the magnitude of the change she had effected in her husband, but they revitalized each other and made the last part of their lives as important as the first. They certainly taught me a lot about life.

I love to tell the story about Mr. Beecher when I speak at nursing homes. You can see the sparks in the eyes of the residents as they consider the possibility of romance. There is no retirement age for love.

ROSEMARY

Twelve years ago I worked as a facilitator in a weight-control program. The group met once a week to check their progress on the scales, to learn about nutrition, and to talk about their experiences as they worked towards their goals.

About five weeks into the course, a strange but very moving thing happened, and it changed the whole way I looked at things. It was after a meeting, while my assistant and I were putting away our teaching aids. I suddenly became aware of someone standing in the back of the auditorium. I looked up and peered out into the darkened room. In the very farthest corner was an enormous woman in a black coat. She seemed kind of spooky.

Then I realized that for five weeks I had been vaguely aware of her presence at the meetings. But she never really came in or joined the group. She never weighed in with the others. She was just always there, on the very outer fringes of the group, like a spectre. Very unsettling.

But this particular night I could see her summoning up every ounce of courage she had, as she began to walk slowly and heavily down the aisle towards me.

I looked at my assistant and asked quietly, "Who is she?"

My assistant said, "I don't know. She usually comes late and leaves early."

The woman finally walked up to where I was standing, and she began to rub her hands together anxiously. Her eyes were downcast, afraid to meet mine. Then she said in a quiet, tremulous voice, "My name is Rosemary. I...I don't know...I don't know if your scale goes high enough ...but I'd really like to see how I'm doing."

I realized at that moment that I was standing face-to-face, person-to-person with another human being who was asking for my help. I looked at this brave woman and said, "Rosemary, we'll figure out something."

We took two scales and carried them down to the boiler room so Rosemary could have some privacy. And there in the basement, that enormous lady stretched out her weight across the two scales. Somehow we got the numbers to match and we discovered that Rosemary had lost 25 pounds since she had been to her doctor at the beginning of our course.

Her great body shook with emotion. I grabbed her massive shoulders and I looked her in the eyes and I said, "Rosemary, I believe in you, and I think we're going to make it." Tears streamed down her face. I cried, too, and we held each other tightly.

Rosemary came to meetings every week after that. Slowly, she began to participate. First she sat in the back row. Then the middle. She began to share her feelings with the group. She told them about how difficult it was for her to begin an exercise program but that she had begun to take long walks outside. Then she began to run. Each week she looked healthier and slimmer. In the spring, she bought a new coat. It was a peach-positive color.

Today, twelve years later, Rosemary works in a department store. She weighs 139 pounds and is no longer frightened.

When she had finally reached her goal, Rosemary said to me, "Janie, you believed in me when I couldn't believe in myself." But what she may not quite understand is that when she put her faith in *me*—when she believed in my ability to help her—she also gave me a gift.

Rosemary and I exchanged the gift of affirmation. When you look at another person with kindness, when you exhibit by your body language, by your touch, by your listening, by your whole being that you believe in her, that you think she has value—then you affirm her worth. And if that person responds to you and puts her trust in you, then you too are affirmed.

Affirmation. It's like a boomerang. It comes back to you.

ENOUGH

A few years ago, I was down in Tennessee doing some work with the Memphis city schools. After my work was done, I decided to take the opportunity one evening to visit some of that city's famous nightspots and to experience firsthand the truly inspirational Southern blues and jazz music I had heard so much about.

I walked into a small club right in the center of Blues Alley. It was pulsating with music and energy—just the type of place I was looking for. I found a seat and settled down in the dim light. The atmosphere was charged with excitement, and at the center of it all was the music.

There was a little yellow-lit stage where musicians jammed in turn, sometimes coming together with remarkable cohesion, sometimes laughing, always enjoying themselves and delighting the crowd of listeners. As the evening progressed, the music got better and better, and around eleven o'clock, I knew the musical meaning of the word "cooking."

Then, suddenly the chatter died and everyone looked towards the doorway. The crowd parted to clear a path to the stage. There was an air of reverence in the room, and I had a wonderful feeling of anticipation. I looked towards the doorway and saw two young black men slowly rolling a very old lady in a wheelchair down the aisle. She smiled a crinkled smile at her admirers as she rolled towards the stage.

The two young men lifted this woman gently from her wheelchair and placed her, in her beautiful old satin evening gown, in a comfortable chair at center stage. Someone handed her a microphone. She had everyone's attention.

Then, in a beautiful Southern drawl, she said, "Ma name is Ma Rainey. I was born right here on Beale Street in Memphis, Tennessee, seventy-eight years ago. I'm seventy-eight years old, and I ain't had nearly enough of nothin' yet!"

That brought the house down.

She sang the old blues songs that night in a clear voice, and joked with her admirers, and glowed with happiness and a love of life.

Later, as I walked slowly home to my hotel room, I thought about her remark that she had not had *enough*. It was clear from her attitude that she was talking about the joyful things in life—music and love and laughter.

I thought about what that word, *enough*, had meant to me in the past. It has always been a very difficult word for me. I have often wondered if, in fact, I was *enough* for the people in my life. Was I a good enough wife, a good enough mother, a good enough speaker? Was I *enough*?

I worried about this a lot, and I spent years trying to assuage my insecurities with artificial comforts, with treats and goodies. But they weren't enough for me. They were never enough. I never did find out exactly how many doughnuts it would take to make me happy. It must have been a great many. But I never did have enough.

I never found out how many scotch-and-sodas it would take, either. Or how much money. None of those things was ever enough to make me happy.

One day I realized that they were *too much*. In fact, I was too much!

In the past six or seven years, my value system has undergone a radical change. Now I know what it takes to make me happy. I heard Ma Rainey at just the right time. I knew what she meant when she said she hadn't had "nearly enough of nothin' yet." She wasn't talking about food or alcohol or *things* of any kind. She was talking about hugs and kisses, pats on the back, beautiful music, and warm love.

She was right. There ain't never *enough* of that.

SHELLY

I could tell right away there was something on Shelly's mind. Something she needed to talk about. I could also tell she was going to make me work for it.

Her long, dark hair hung down the sides of her pale face, as if she could hide behind it. But she could not hide her eyes—angry, frightened, beautiful eyes. Hurt, too.

Shelly hunched down in a dejected, defensive position. Cross-legged, she made a little ball of herself, her chin supported in her hands, her elbows supported on her knees, as she sat with ten other teenagers in a circle on the floor of the high school lounge. All of these kids had gone through treatment for chemical dependency, some without success. I came to the school to talk with them, to try to touch them with a little love and understanding if they would let me. Sometimes they do. Sometimes they surprise me.

"Hi, Shelly," I said.

Shelly grunted something that I was supposed to accept as a greeting.

"How's it going?" I asked.

"It's not going at all," was the bitter reply.

"Well, what's happening?" I pressed.

Shelly straightened. She looked angry, and her anger gave her strength.

"School sucks," she spat. "For that matter, everything sucks! And I hate my mother."

Her anger went deeper than her words, and I felt for her. She looked to me like an animal caught in a trap.

"Why do you say that?"

"Well, now on top of everything else, she says she wants me to quit smoking."

"Oh. Do you want to smoke?"

Shelly glared at me defiantly. "No," she replied, "but I'm not just going to do everything SHE says. What does she want from me? I've been through treatment three times already. I don't have to quit smoking, too."

"But if you don't want to smoke, why smoke?"

Shelly sighed impatiently and did not answer.

"Well, what are you going to do?" I asked.

She seemed startled by the question so I elaborated. "If you're mad at your mother because she wants you to quit smoking, what are you going to do about it?"

Shelly shook her hair back from her face, her eyes now rebellious. "I'm going over to my boyfriend's house to spend the weekend with him...in bed!"

"Hm," I said making it clear that Shelly still had not shocked me. "You know, Shelly, you were able to give up drugs and booze already. It's tough. Maybe you will give up smoking, too. I wonder if having sex with your boyfriend is a sort of substitute for those other things?"

Those beautiful dark eyes were so confused.

"But here's what I think," I continued. "I think that you're not going to sleep with your boyfriend this weekend. I think you're not going to smoke or do anything like that."

"Oh, yeah?" Shelly challenged, rising up, her hands planted firmly on her hips. "So what AM I going to do, then?"

I tried to ignore her belligerence. "I think that Friday night's going to come along, and you're going to feel kind of lonely. I think you'll pick up the phone and call 555-4058 and then you're going to say, 'Janie J.? This is Shelly. I feel real lonely and I feel real scared. Could I come over and sit on your blue couch and could I have a hug?'"

"Well, that's stupid!" Shelly spit out. "I'm not going to do that!" And she stomped away from the group, throwing her head back, swinging her arms with exaggerated confidence.

Friday night came and I was at home reading. At eleven o'clock, the phone rang and a little voice said "Janie J.? This is Shelly. I feel real scared and I feel real lonely and I don't just want to sleep with my boyfriend. I really want to be straight and do things differently. I don't want to smoke. I don't want to drink. Could I come over and sit on your blue couch? And could I have a hug?"

BEIGE

My grandmother, Sarah Jane Flannigan, a beautiful, talented woman, struggled her whole life with being overweight. She had three daughters, Edna, Jennie and Pearl. They, too, struggled their whole lives with being overweight. Pearl, my mother, had one daughter—me. I have struggled my whole life with being overweight. Finally, I think I have discovered the family secret—the fatal family mistake. The key to the Flannigan Flab. The women in my family only know how to cook and eat in the color *beige*.

My grandmother thought a well-balanced meal consisted of bratwurst, mashed potatoes, creamed corn and custard pie. All beige. Much too much beige.

If you are eating more beige than you should be eating, you are probably rounder than you want to be. So, what you need to do is simply cut down on your beige-intake. This is a little like the best-selling COLOR ME BEAUTIFUL. You must be honest about your color assessment. Beige covers a wide range of the spectrum from cream colors to buff to tan to mocha to taupe.

I must admit that the meals I prefer to eat usually include an extraordinary amount of beige. Think of all the foods there are in beige. Fresh coffee cake with a little honey sauce dripping down. Pecan rolls that stick to your fingers. Those caramels you find while you sit watching television—removing paper after paper and folding the papers and stacking them neatly to one side. When you get up to change the channel during a commercial, you might throw away the papers and then you don't really have any idea how many you've eaten.

Beige is, in fact, the color of the most appealing and comforting foods we were weaned on. Pablum, strained applesauce, graham crackers, peanut butter, toast, and warm, yummy cocoa.

Beige is potato chips leaping out of the bag as if they're attached to one another like Rosary beads and fairly leaping into your mouth one right after the other.

Beige. So dangerous.

There are some stories about terrible beige problems people can have. For instance, there's the sad saga of Gail and almond bark at Christmas time. When Gail got a new microwave oven, she became excited at the prospect of all the wonderful candies and treats she could make in it for Christmas. Her microwave cookbook suggested melting almond bark down to a creamy sauce, and dipping various foods into it to make little almond-coated candies. So Gail went off to the store and bought bag after bag of almond bark and melted it down in her new microwave oven. Then she began to dip things like cake cubes into the almond bark and dry them out on a paper towel. She dipped cherries and breads, as her cookbook suggested. But then she got carried away. She dipped pretzels and corn curls. She dipped zucchini and liverwurst. She dipped pork chops. Soon everything in her refrigerator was coated with a thin, sweet shell of beige. There was an endless supply of Christmas treats. But the trouble was that Gail ended up eating them endlessly. Poor Gail gained seventeen pounds in the two weeks before Christmas and all because of the irresistible color beige.

And there is the story of my friend Barb, who had a tremendous beige attack every time she drove past— or shall I say TRIED to drive past—the Golden Arches. She could never resist buying those famous beige french fries. Her car would veer into the drive-through lane as though it had a mind of its own. She knew her obsession with the french fries had reached dangerous proportions when she wrote out a check for fifty-two cents the day she came up short! Now Barb drove around town a lot on her job and she would be confronted with a McDonald's three or four times in a single day. Although she liked her job, Barb found she was getting rounder and rounder. She quit her job and took an office job that would keep her away from the beige bits. On her resignation she listed as her reason for leaving—beige. *McBeige* to be precise!

One man wrote me from a town in Minnesota, "Would a Peanut Buster Bar from Dairy Queen count as beige?"

Yes, and chocolate is the most dangerous shade of beige.

I have a daughter named Janet who is five feet, eight inches tall, weighs 126 pounds and never struggles with being overweight. She broke our family tradition with a secret of her own. Number one, she never eats too much beige. Number two, she never eats too much.

MATTHEW

What in the world was I going to say to a group of Ojibwa Indian parents that was going to make any sense at all? I mean, what about me was at all RELEVANT to life in a Duluth, Minnesota Indian community?

"Frankie, will you just tell me WHY it is that I get myself into these things that I'm totally unprepared for?" I know I must have appeared ruffled, because immediately Frankie began to console me. It worked for a while, but soon enough, my anxieties re-appeared. I was afraid of how I might be accepted by people whose culture was different from my own.

So I started to fret about other things to mask my distress.

"I'm so TIRED!" I complained to Frankie. Of course she was keeping the same schedule as I was, so I couldn't have been any more tired than she. And SHE wasn't whining.

Then I decided to blame the weather, an easy scapegoat in Minnesota. "It's APRIL!" I moaned. "And it's so cold and gray! I want spring! I can't stand it!" Almost as if in answer to my plea, the sky exploded into a perverse burst of snow flurries. Frankie wisely took over the driving while I fussed and grumbled beside her. She knew I was apprehensive. What could we possibly give these people? Was it really important for us to be there?

Just before we entered the building where the hundred or so parents were supposed to be assembled, I figured I'd better adjust my attitude. I decided this was my big opportunity to reach out to others in understanding and we'd all be brothers and sisters in love. Yeah. That's it. I could do it.

So Frankie and I pulled ourselves together. There we were, expectant and energetic.

I placed my collection of props near the front of the room, and looked out over my audience, sixteen people, scattered randomly among the chairs. In the front row sat a young woman and her little boy. Great! I was called up here to talk to a parents' group, and who shows up but a *kid*!

Oh, I tell you, by this time I had worked myself into the bum attitude of the century.

Almost as if he could sense my discomfort, the child began to squirm. I tried to give my speech but my glance kept getting sidetracked by the little boy's antics. He was all over the place; he crawled under the chair, over the chair, over his mother, and I just couldn't concentrate. He tugged at his mother and she kept saying "SH!" He went to the potty three times. Why, I asked myself, did his mother bring him to a meeting for adults?

I tried to look over his head; my focus kept returning to his perpetual motion.

Just as I was making a very important point, he made a terrible face and then burst into giggles. He saw my face, and realized I was becoming impatient with him so he began to settle down.

I thought, "What am I going to do with this kid?" And then I realized I could USE him. A living, squirming prop!

I cleared my throat and said, "Oh, Ma'am?" to the child's mother.

"Yes?"

"Could I please borrow your little boy? I seem to have misplaced my 'little boy' prop."

Bewildered, the mother led the child over to where I stood and we all sat down and faced the audience.

"Your name?" I asked the boy.

"Matthew."

I hadn't noticed before that he was a sweet, gentle little boy. Now I felt ashamed at my impatience with him. I held my hand out to the boy, half afraid he would not take it because he had seen my displeasure before. But he brightened with the instant forgiveness given to children and toddled over to hold my hand. His tiny hands were warm; his smile flashed. He was by far the most alive thing in the room.

"Well, Matthew," I said. "I'd like you to help me tell my tree story. Would you get my tree?" He carried over the Norfolk pine I carried with me in hopes that I would tell my tree story enough times to see it grow to full maturity. Matthew was now infused with a great sense of self-importance.

"Now do you think this is a baby tree or a grown-up tree?"

"Oh, a baby tree."

We talked about trees and how they compare to people. The little boy was delighted to think about trees being Daddies and Mommies and Aunts and Grandpas.

"Big trees say to little ones, 'Lean with us...we know you are small and scared but we'll protect you. You are our little trees and we believe in you.'"

Matthew and his mother liked that. I found myself overcome with feeling for this small boy. "Nothing is as lovely as a little pine tree, Matthew, except perhaps the precious beauty of a child," I said filled with emotion.

The others in the audience were moved by the boy, too. As parents, they too had rediscovered with me the glory of a child through Matthew...that glory we so often brush aside. At the end of the program, all sixteen people made a circle around the boy and sang, "Love Makes the World Go 'Round."

Matthew reached out his little hand and touched every person as they walked by, innocent and trusting. His smile broke down the barriers between the cultures—between the ages. We parted, all the richer for his presence.

#   #   #

A month later, I received this letter:

Dear Janie,

The day you spent with us in Duluth was one of my most cherished days. The presentation was wonderful and I feel compelled to write to you.

You thanked me that day for providing the group with a 'prop.' My son and I were in the first row. When I think of that day I remember it as one of the special times he and I spent together.

After you were here, my son came down with a virus and no matter what the doctors did, they could not save him. He passed away in his sleep. I picture him now in the forest of heaven with our relatives around him. Our children are only lent to us and I am enclosing the church bulletin from his service to show you.

Thank you again for one of the most beautiful days in my son's and in my life.

Matthew's mother

STUFF

The group of people was milling about outside the auditorium where I was scheduled to speak. I was milling with them, *incognito* in my sunglasses, listening to their comments. (It hadn't occurred to me that the disguise was unnecessary; no one knew who I was anyway...) One man, naturally not knowing that I was to be the program speaker, murmured to me, "This 'motivational speaker'—do you suppose she's one of those 'touchie-feelie' types?"

I pushed my glasses up onto my head—voila!—and took his hand in both of mine. "You *bet* I am," I smiled.

Everyone knows the warm comfort we exchange when we experience physical contact with another person. Studies have been done in which the emotional benefits of touching were revealed. Dr. Richard Seiden of the University of California, and anthropologist Dr. Ashley Montagu both suggest that touching, hugging and sensory expression can lead to better emotional health.

So why do we hold back? It probably has a lot to do with the "body self." People keep others from them because of their bodies. Maybe they feel they just don't have the right "stuff."

When I was newly single after so many years of being married, I felt untouched. My skin felt deprived, my soul detached from my body.

A friend and confidante, Sister Paula, taught me a special secret.

"Every morning when you are in the shower," she told me, "imagine each part of your body and the good it brings to you. Touch your head with massaging fingertips, smooth your eyelids, pat your face, acknowledge your throat, place your hands on your heart and your diaphragm, while taking a big breath of life. Pat your tummy and tell it, 'let's eat good, nutritious food this day.' Smooth your knees, and reach down and give your toes a squeeze."

Acknowledging your body as a part of your being, blessing it and affirming it, gives you insights to the goodness of your body self.

Instead of constantly thinking about how great you'll look when you lose ten more pounds, take a look in the mirror. That's your "stuff." Enjoy it and love it, and in the process, give it better nutrition, more exercise, more sleep.

Give your body this treat: When you go home tonight, go to your bedroom and take off all those constricting clothes, those starchy shirts and neckties. Those tight bras and girdles. Put on your big old muu-muu or robe and go outside in the backyard and just roll around in the grass! Do it real late at night, so your neighbors won't see you. If they do and they think you look stupid, just tell them, "Janie Jasin MADE me do this."

It's your body; it's your stuff.

With our bodies, we are always showing to others how we feel, whether we want to admit it or not. Think of your body language. The "doormat" body language, for instance—your shoulders droop, your stomach hangs out and you look like such a sufferer, as if to say, "Strap another load on me; *I* don't mind!" Or the "I've had it!" body language—tight fists, tight stomach, tight thighs, tight buttocks.

Your body speaks for you.

You can understand how important your body's expression is when you are suddenly deprived of it.

About three years ago I met a man who worked with stroke victims. Jack told me about his unusual and very successful ideas for therapy. He would walk into the patients' room and get into their bed with them, assuming the shapes they had in their pain, and asking them if he could speak for them. The words that came out of his mouth in those circumstances were words like, "If your body were shaped like mine, you'd cry, too! You'd be ornery and you'd throw things, too!" When they saw and heard him speaking for them, they felt such relief.

It seems to me that those who have been touched by pain have developed deep compassion and empathy for others who suffer.

We need to affirm our bodies, no matter what condition they are in. No matter if they are sick or well, young or old, fat or thin. And we need to affirm the bodies of others as well.

On a recent visit home, I shared a quiet moment with my very old Aunt Jennie, my dear godmother—a wonderful lady full of fun and joy—now 82. I was helping her with her bath, soaping her skin with bubbles and washing under her fallen breasts with a cloth. Knowing my aunt's spunky nature, I motioned to her bosom and asked her, "Aunt Jennie, just how big WERE those in their day?"

Aunt Jennie smiled, sat up, lifted her chin, and boasted, "I was a 38-D, honey. Now will you please hand me my Jean Nate."

It's your stuff. It's your body self. Acknowledge it, affirm it, love it. The world could use a little more "touchie-feelie."

CHANGE

I rebel against change. It's so uncomfortable for me. And I just HATE discomfort. The older I get, the more comfort I crave.

Someone says to me, "Hey, want to go bowling?"

Without even considering the possibility, I immediately respond, "Oh, no. No. I can't change my plans."

"Oh. What do you have planned?"

In my mind, I know what I have planned. My evening is all mapped out. I cannot change. I plan to lie on the couch and watch television under my old afghan and overeat. But I can't SAY that! I'll have to say something else.

"Plans, yes. Well, I plan to have company (the dog)."

"Swell! Why don't you invite your company to go along? We can ALL go bowling!"

I've backed myself into a corner. I suppose it

wouldn't require a tremendous amount of effort to go out with my friends. But BOWLING! Why did they have to suggest bowling? I haven't bowled in years. I probably can't bowl. I *don't* bowl. Nope. My mother never bowled, my father never bowled, and I don't bowl, either.

And so I spent the evening with the dog and the TV and the afghan, feeling vaguely angry and eating a lot of beige-colored snacks, putting back on the two pounds I had lost last week, and losing the self-esteem I had gained. All because I refused to make a small change, to take a small risk.

But little by little, I'm learning. It's hard, no question about that. The most important lesson I learned is that it becomes a lot easier when you decide to ask others for help. They really will help, but you have to ask first.

It's so hard to say, "Could somebody please help me? I need help." It sounds like you're weak, vulnerable. But it was the help from friends given to me when I finally asked for it that enabled me to successfully change my destructive behavior.

In 1969, I had run out of dreams. I could no longer fool myself into thinking I was fine. One morning I stepped onto the bathroom scale and read the numbers in disbelief. I weighed 251 pounds! I was thirty years old. I was so frightened by this that I ran out into my backyard and stood, alone, by the big elm tree, in a panic. I knew I needed help in order to change my life. So I prayed. "Please, God, help me to be normal; help me to change." This was my first honest request for help.

And slowly, I began to change. All my friends and family members encouraged me, and the whole effort gained momentum. With every step I took, I found more and more help, both spiritual and personal.

I began doing some things that were very hard for me. I went to Sears and bought an Extra Large jogging suit. (The very fact that the store carried jogging suits that size I viewed as encouragement.) I started to jog around the neighborhood. Soon my neighbors began to call to me, "Hey, go for it, Janie!" and "We're with you all the way Janie J.!"

The jogging itself was so hard. Besides fatigue, I had to cope with chafed thighs, AND with the embarrassingly loud swishing noise my pants inseams made from the friction.

It was not easy. But I learned to stick to a 500-calorie-a-day diet. I joined a modern dance class. I recorded everything I ate, every last calorie. I adopted different behavior patterns. In other words, I *changed*.

Miraculously, the weight started to come off. With the aid of my friends who became my supporters, I continued to change both my eating and my exercise habits.

I remember jogging down the main street of my little town, and running up to the bakery door, swinging the door wide open and calling in to whoever was there, "See? I'm not buying anything!" Even the baker, although he was losing possibly his best customer, cheered me on.

Encouragement is something that I always respond to. I guess most of us do. I heard a terrific speaker last year, a psychologist named John Brantner. He said that one of the nicest things to have in your life is someone who loves you enough to LIE CONVINCINGLY. Someone who, when you are at your worst, will tell you, "You're doing O.K. You're going to make it!" You need that help in order to change.

I was invited to speak at a church in Minnesota—a small community church. When I got there, I was surprised to notice that all the people sat in the back third of the church. I turned to the pastor, and whispered, "What's the deal, Father? Why do all the people sit crowded together in the back pews?"

The priest smiled and said, "Well, their mothers sat back there, and their fathers sat back there..."

I said, "Father, what do you do for the Mass?"

He said, "I do the only thing I can do—I carry the altar down to them."

It's really hard to change human behavior. It is so uncomfortable. Scary. But real comfort comes in changing your habits out of respect for yourself and your own worth.

And, I promise, the next time they ask me to go bowling, I'm gonna go.

BLOOMING PRAIRIE, MN 55917

In the midst of one of Minnesota's classic, block-buster blizzards, I drove my faltering automobile down a dark and winding rural ribbon of roadway towards Blooming Prairie, Minnesota, where I was scheduled to address a group of people in a country church. Twenty miles outside of town, my car, the Wimpmobile, declared its motor The Little Engine That Couldn't.

Why tonight, in the middle of this blustery snowstorm?

And why Blooming Prairie, a little hinterland hamlet nobody had ever heard of, out in the middle of Nowhere, USA? BLOOMING PRAIRIE! A likely name. Who were they kidding; nothing could possibly bloom here! More apt would have been Frozen Tundra, Minnesota. Perhaps the township had been named by some displaced Englishman on just such a night as this one—when the poor fellow cursed the blasted, blooming prairie!

Anyway, this wasn't getting me anywhere. I was much closer to Blooming Prairie than I was to Minneapolis, so I had to hitch a ride into town, although I doubted anyone would be there to hear my speech. I got out of the car and stood in the road, a vision in my little red high-heels, holding a white dinner jacket swinging on a hanger in one hand, and a box of props in the other. I must have looked like the mother of the bride arriving late for her daughter's June wedding. I clicked the frozen heels of those little red shoes together and thought to myself, "There's no place like home; there's no place like home."

Sure enough, my prayers were answered. Well, not really. Unlike Dorothy, I didn't wake up at home, but a motorist stopped to pick me up. I think the waving dinner jacket flagged her down.

The driver beckoned me into the car, and after questioning me about my destination, she said. "I know where that church is located. I'll take you there." I seemed to be riding on waves of fate that evening so I gave myself up to it.

The woman drove me to the church and dropped me off, bidding me a warm good night. I hurried inside and found 250 people gathered for the ecumenical dinner. Suddenly, I no longer felt it strange that all these people would brave a winter night storm for such a meeting. There was a real warmth radiating from these folks that melted the feeling of isolation that the Arctic storm had imposed on me.

The priest, Father Ginther, ushered me to a table and introduced me to an assortment of ministers and their families, gave me a slice of cherry pie, and then settled down to listen to the musical program presented by the children's choir.

I breathed heavily with a strange relief as I listened to the kids sing their angelic hymns. *Relief*, despite the fact that I was miles from home, without a car, a toothbrush, a nightie, a place to sleep. I felt somehow safe and among loving people. I relaxed.

My plan had been to scurry down to Blooming Prairie, do the speech, hurry home, and get the next day's activities going. But I had been detoured. I was, in fact, stopped. Maybe there was a purpose for me to be in Blooming Prairie.

The choir program concluded, Father Ginther introduced me with warm wit and I was on. My heart needing peace, I impulsively scrapped the rehearsed speech and began to talk to these people in earnest. I spoke about feelings so close to my heart that I had never before allowed them to be divulged before a group. I told them painful things about destructive behavior and low self-esteem. And I told them joyful things about affirming love and about heartfelt communication with others. We reached out to one another. My speech ended and the precious people of Blooming Prairie rose to their feet and applauded.

People came up to me after the talk to chat with me. Their manner was friendly, personal, not removed as city crowds can sometimes be. They all seemed to be concerned with my car problems.

"What did the car sound like? Where is it? May I have your keys?"

The men went off. Father Ginther and I followed Ann, the housekeeper, into the rectory parlor. We talked, we shared, we relaxed. Again, that strange sense of well-being settled over me, despite my being isolated in the middle of "nowhere." Father Ginther spoke with much love about his parishioners. I saw such goodness and gentleness in this man. But he was worried about the problems that beset his congregation. He was particularly worried about selfishness.

Two hours passed. The self-appointed mechanics appeared at the door. One of them held up my keys. "Your car is ready," he said. "Repaired, carburetor cleaned, ready to go. It'll run great for you." Somehow, I knew it would.

I drove the man who fixed my car back to his shop. He protested when I tried to reimburse him for his efforts. "No, you don't have to pay me, lady. I didn't mind fixing your car. I didn't have that much to do today anyways. My wife's mother just passed away and I wasn't that busy, because of the funeral plans. Just hearing your speech was pay enough. I really didn't mind working on your car. I'm going into auto repair full-time now because of the layoffs at the company I work for."

As the man and I drove along a dark stretch of open road at midnight, he looked over to a particular spot on the side of the road and said, "This is where my sixteen-year-old son was killed by a drunken driver."

My heart stopped, and I knew at that moment why I had gone to Blooming Prairie, Minnesota. I had gone to *speak* so that I could hear. And I heard clearly. It could have been *me* seven years ago, driving drunk down that highway. It could have been me who killed someone's son. *It could have been me.*

He didn't appear to be depressed by the blows he had been dealt. Rather, this man knew how to cope, with a glorious optimism that was infectious.

I gave the man a poem I had written about my struggle with alcoholism. I saw the tears in his eyes through the tears in my own. It was all so strange. I had never met this man but he was somehow familiar, as was the whole town.

I felt grateful that I was alive. I was blessed to be sober. I was blessed to be clean and serene. I was twice blessed to have been in Blooming Prairie, Minnesota.

FLAGS

During the last few minutes before a recent presentation, I was busily arranging my props on a small table at the front of the auditorium. Just the bare essentials this time: crepe-paper hearts, scratch-and-sniff chocolates, silver tap shoes, my lavendar satin turban with its accompanying wisdom, and seventeen brightly colored flags. An odd assortment, I agree, but the tools of my trade nonetheless.

Usually, when people see these strange items on display before a program, they tend to become bewildered, and they whisper and point, and I imagine they are saying things like, "What in the world have we gotten ourselves into?"

Well, this one time, as I smoothed out the flags, an elderly gentleman approached me wearing a huge grin. He looked excitedly from one prop to another and then at me, saying, "Oh, just look at all these wonderful things! We're going to march around and wave the flags, aren't we? Oh, we ARE going to have a lot of fun!"

I use flag props for various role-playing exercises to shed inhibitions, to identify behavior, and, well, just to have fun. Flags and banners and emblems and signs are very expressive and they help people to make statements about themselves. People display their flags to show patriotism, to elicit nostalgia, to make announcements, to get attention. Little children love to wave flags. So do great nations. So does my dad.

Oh, now, my dad doesn't spend his days marching around the neighborhood waving little flags. He's quite dignified about it actually. He has an impressive collection of flags and banners, each commemorating certain special events or memories that he holds dear.

Dad used to fly his flags from poles set into the sandy beach at our summer cottage. We'd look like the United Nations, or a used Chevy dealership, or something.

People would go by and ask, "What are the flags for?" And my dad would say, "I don't know. Why don't we start something?"

And he would. He is a gifted organizer, and he'd start some great community activity that would invariably snowball, and end in great fun for him and everybody else. Just because he had set out his flags.

Of course, some of these events didn't turn out as well as others. But some turned out real well. Like the Silver Lake Water Ski Show he promoted one summer in the 50s at an old resort in Wisconsin where we were staying.

It was Memorial Day weekend, and it was rainy and cold. The summer hadn't even properly begun yet, and everyone was bored and cranky.

This would never do, my dad thought, so he went quietly to his room and retrieved his collection of flags. Very carefully, he went outside and began to plant them in a row on the lawn in front of the old resort. It was obvious to us that he was planning to "start something."

"Go ask your mother for three shirt cardboards, Janie, like a good girl," he told me.

I ran inside to execute my mission. By now, my mother had ceased to be astonished at my dad's eccentric requests. She had no idea whatsoever why he needed them, but she miraculously produced the shirt cardboards just the same.

Dad was beginning to draw a crowd of interested onlookers. "What are the flags for?" asked one brave soul.

I handed my dad the shirt cardboards, and he took a red crayon from his back pocket. Everyone watched as he wrote announcements on each cardboard. One said BEAUTY QUEEN CONTEST. The second read BOAT PARADE, and the third, WATER SKI SHOW.

All at once, the onlookers gasped. They never once doubted my dad's authority over such events, plus they were all so pleased to have something to look forward to on this bleak holiday weekend.

Dad hung the announcements on the foyer wall of the old resort and began to organize the activities. People came up to him and asked "When? Where?" and "Can I help?"

My dad described to them the celebration that he said would occur on Labor Day. He could see it all before his very eyes. He had wonderful vision.

"On Labor Day," he proclaimed, "we're going to have a marvelous boat parade, so get your boats all decked out. Tell your talented children to practice all their water skiing tricks for the ski show. There'll be ten wonderful acts. And enter your beautiful daughters in the beauty contest."

Then my dad began organizing committees. The gangs of teenagers who had hung about listlessly were suddenly infused with the spirit of friendly competition, as they polished and tuned their boats and canoes. The children and parents were active in preparing their water ski tricks. And even the old-timers were called on by my dad to participate. In fact, they got the plum assignment.

"Would you guys like to have the honor of judging the beauty contest?" he diplomatically asked the old curmudgeons. So taken aback and flattered were they that they forgot to be too crabby to join in the festivities.

Labor Day finally arrived and the day shone sunny and warm, just as my dad had planned. The panel of distinguished judges sat out on the beach by the row of flags and solemnly chose a queen from among the thirteen beautiful girls who had registered for the contest.

The water ski show, featuring well-practiced family acts, was a rousing success.

And the boat show featured 50 vessels of all types and sizes, decorated with what seemed like hundreds of flags, led by a pontoon boat with a full orchestra on board.

Nearly 2,000 people from all over the area came to the show. Someone had made up a little song about my dad and the Silver Lake Ski Show to demonstrate the residents' appreciation to him for "starting something" that had turned out to be so wonderful.

One day last summer, years now since the Silver Lake Ski Show, I was feeling very lonely.

I thought about my dad, and about his collection of flags flying on the lake shore. He had given me several of the flags—my favorites—since that festival summer. I remembered where I had stored them, and I went and got them. I brought the red one out to the front yard where I now live, and skewered it into my lawn. A little boy came by and asked me, "What's the flag for?"

I said to him, "I don't know. Maybe we ought to start something."

The little boy was enthusiastic. "A picnic!" he suggested. "A picnic for the whole neighborhood!"

That afternoon, we miraculously produced a wonderful neighborhood picnic supper, with music and laughter and friendship. The whole scene reminded me of my dad's joyful spontaneity, and I missed him. I went in the house to telephone. My mother answered.

"Is Daddy home?" I asked.

"No," she answered. "He's over at his store."

"What's he doing there at this time of night?"

My mother chuckled softly and answered, "He's putting up his flags."

Short Pieces

Success is...

Success is the feeling you get when you know
You did something so special, you were the star of your show.
It's a fire that crackles and feels like it glows
You get all excited right down through your toes.
It makes you so peppy, you can hardly sit still.
Your mind dances around you from ridges to rill.
You speak with conviction YOU BELIEVE IN YOURSELF.
You say what you're thinking, you jump off your shelf.
The people you meet stay on just to listen.
They stay all around you to learn how to glisten.
And later that day when you are alone.
You find that you're smiling right through to the bone.
For success is the service, turned into esteem.
You did something for others, your lamp's on high beam.
You look on ahead not frightened or shy.
You can see more good coming, you know by and by.
That you've got what it takes to build on the past
Remembering highlights and memories that last.
Putting others out front, you turn inside out.
You feel what they're feeling. Their praises you shout.
You wrap it in presents, and still you get more.
You draw it in pictures, it comes in the door.
You keep on giving it and giving it away.
But success keeps on coming, and it stays and it stays
And it stays. CALLIGRAPHER · DIANE M. VON ARX

Alone For Awhile

I've been alone for a while now. The duel has ended. I have laid down the sword and marked the ground with peaceful thoughts. He has gone his way and chosen a new mate. I choose the aloneness for strength and healing.

I do not regret these years of aloneness. They were not lonely years. They were climbing years. Each step up, further from dependence and conflict and sorrow and pain and tears.

The dog and I with our places set and TV rattling nearby. A neighbor stopping with news and chatter. A client calling. A co-worker phoning. Classes to teach, people to reach, a God to beseech.

Alone, God and I and the dog and neighbors and friends and family. A daughter one phone call, a town, away. Near enough just in case I need to find out if I'm still a Mom. A son in town growing up, to summon if needed.

A son with his Dad, more painful to reach, for it connects the past pain with present growth and leaves me powerless again.

I've been alone with God these days of growth. He and I making our pact. God saying, "I love you. I am with you. I will never abandon you."

I research the Scriptures:
And God said, "It is not good for man to be alone. I will send him a helpmate."

So . . . what did God say to the woman? "Woman! Woman!" I cannot hear what God says to do. Could it be there are no rules for women alone?

I say to myself, "You are some kind of woman, Janie J, with goodness and life and strength and caring — *Give of Yourself!* Reach out and touch the world!"

His eye is on the sparrow. He watches. Let not you be carried away with your own wonder: Give that wonder to those without hope. This time, this wondrous time I've had, to be ALONE.

I've learned.
I've learned the value of a kiss.
I've learned the value of an embrace.
I've learned the value of a hand clasp.
I've learned to take care of me without conflict. Inside my gentle self, an urging that said, "You're doing it — the bills — the mortgage — the tires — the payments — the car — the career."

Oh, my gosh, I laugh to myself. Why did I think it was so impossible? Numbers and tires and payments and work weren't the hard part.

The hard part was . . . TRUST and BELIEF that I was CAPABLE.

Higher Power

Power greater than mine come into me.
Power greater than mine to heal me, come through me.
Power greater than mine, move into me.
Power greater than mine, still my negative thinking.
Surround me . . . unfold my presence, through my gifts
    to others.
Open my world and make it available to those near me.
Spin my mind into whirling, wonderful, creative
    thought patterns.
Unravel the snarl of ugly resentments.
Weave the best of me into a tapestry of warmth and
    comforting.
Begin my endings with forgiveness, end my resentments
    with loving.
Start my heart again, fill it up with premium love.
Unlock the cold bitterness with touch and healing.
I want to feel the pain and euphoria of life and what it is.
Take away the numbness of justification.
I am only who I am and no one more.
Unfurl the flag of surrender, wave it with a flourish, and
    fly it for all to see: I didn't quit. I surrendered, not to
    my will but to Thy will.
May it be done.

She Was Twenty-One Yesterday

There she was. My little bundle of yesterday, all grown up and walking toward me. She and her college roommate and her dearest friend from childhood. They walked toward the maitre d', where I waited in the elegant French cafe.

Janet, 5'8", in a scooped-neck dress with a sash of watercolor blue drawn about her waist, with blonde hair flowing here and there in curly fluff (except where a pastel ribbon smoothed its flow), walked to me with a swish.

I couldn't believe it had happened. She had become a woman with verve and sparkle and inner bounce — like a puppet on rubber bands.

We dined together and I looked around at the table and into these young women's eyes. I realized she had brought her best friends.

I remembered Janet's father proposing to me when I was the age of these three women. I recalled the birthday parties of days past: the little girls looking at party favors, balloons and prizes with eagerness and wonder. Today we dined on escargot and French delicacies, and oohed and aahed at candlelight, music and elegance.

The best part of it was that she wanted me to go dancing with her friends after dinner. I was horrified, thinking of strangers staring at me, a forty-six-year-old mom trying to keep up with youth. I should have known it wouldn't be that way.

We arrived at the night spot. The three young ladies grabbed hands and jumped onto the dance floor where they bobbed to the tunes together.

There were no pick-ups, no preparatory drinking, just the three of them delighting to the music, dancing together. It was obvious that the other dancers and spectators accepted these three young ladies whirling about together.

Then it happened. The trio said, "Come on, Mom. Come *on,* Mom!" So I moved into the crowd. I joined them, and bobbed along with them. I found out it was not so different from the days when Janet and I exercised in the living room together or danced those old steps (my steps) of the Fifties.

I joined them and enjoyed them and no one gasped or gaped or jeered at my forty-six-year-old legs dancing. We danced with joy and glee the night Janet was twenty-one.

I wouldn't have missed it for the world. She was the most beautiful girl in the room. I know, because I'm her mom and I love her.

I'll always be grateful that those years ago — so few, so many — I had a blue-eyed, blonde-haired bundle in Falls Church, Virginia. She weighed in at 7 pounds, 9 ounces.

> *We named her*
> *Janet Katherine Jasin*
> *and yesterday she was*
> *Twenty-One.*

The Separation

At the end there were no tears,
 just a tired ache and a feeling of sad nothingness,
for all of the years and all of the times that were supposed
to be A Love Story.
The girl from long ago that believed a man could do
anything. The boy from long ago that thought girls were
all like Mom and soft and sexy and forever.

There were so many joys, like looking at three newborn
faces and knowing half of that was yours and half was
mine.
The days of first dinners and champagne, the cards and
presents, the raises and the new jobs, the first teeth,
the fevers in the night, and the waiting.
The waiting for the the end of sailing trips, hunting, scuba,
sales trips; and the waiting for love.
And all the time you waited too.
For diapers to be folded, dust to be vacuumed, a career
to take shape, a woman to be born out of a chemically
dependent person.
And you waited for her to be what you needed
and it didn't happen.

The anger of not having it happen is explosive,
headache-making, lonely.
The pain of Hell on Earth, and the loss of hope, the

knowing that there aren't hugs or kisses from another being, a committed being, and the wanting them, the wonder if . . . there ever will be again?

Today I am sorry for all of the things I wasn't when you needed them.
Today I am certain that I've hurt you so many times.
Today I am relieved that I don't have to try and "make it better" all alone.
Thank you for the understanding and the admission that it is "no-fault." God, I needed to know that I wasn't all alone in all of it.

And in the end it was like the lake at sunset, calm, serene, and leveling. I will always remember the lake and that you gave me the dream. The fact that you gave me something no one else ever did is really something. You gave me a lot of things like that: three children, three dogs, a white house with black shutters and
a chance to be me.
Thank you.
Janie

Brief-case Barbies

Are you out there in Business Land, competing and complaining and working and managing and dying early — like the men? Women are out there in their three-piece suits, wearing pretend neckties, wanting to play the game the same as the men do. Thinking they *need* to play the business game in order to be important, in order to be real. Defining themselves by the corporate values and the corporate rules.

Ladies, let's be feminine and competent, and encourage the men to be competent and gentlemen.

In Fargo-Moorhead, South Dakota, I spoke to a group of banking women. Dr. Joyce Brothers was hired to speak there also. I noticed the high-pitched excitement of the women as they bunched up to make the big self-introduction to *Dr. Joyce Brothers.*

Dr. Joyce Brothers was someone they admired, someone they wanted to impress — to make an impression on. So they puffed up and held their chins up, and went up to her, saying in their biggest voices, "Oh, Dr. Brothers, I've been in banking 23 years, "Oh, Dr. Brothers, I'm an MBA in the CBB," "Dr. Brothers, I've been in banking since the dollar was first printed," "Dr. Brothers, I'm a senior VP in the MMC, a member of the BBC and the AIB and the CIA."

I laughed to myself. I watched all of these women struggling to be Big Deals. Then I went over to Dr. Brothers, and simply said, "Joyce, my name is Janie. I'm a person."

Joyce sighed and said, "Thank God."

WHY IS IT THAT WHEN WE ARE OURSELVES IT MAKES LIFE SO MUCH EASIER?

. . . true identity . . .
it is found in creative activity
springing from within.

Anne Morrow Lindbergh

Parenting My Parents

This disease...this baffling journey into lost memories has me in arms as I struggle to make sense of my parents last years.

It was acceptable, so I thought, to take Daddy's mind and twist it into a mess. I could get through that with effort and stamina and TLC administered from a city 7 hours away from where he suffered. I could catch a plane and be there for activities and watch him refuse to throw a velcro ball.

That day, that spring April day when I entered the activity room and saw him my heart sank into a purple hole. Then I moved in close and said. . . Come on Daddy let's do it. . .I clapped and he threw it onto a perfect bulls eye.

I clapped for him as he had clapped for me the day I rode a two wheeler, dressed for the prom, water skied for the first time and gave birth to three grandchildren. He clapped for 40 years and I clapped for his last years.

He was gone in May "87" lost to Alzheimers. His mind, his, spirit and his vitality was robbed.

While Bob Hope performed in the Persian Gulf my Daddy who would have been the same age was lost. It wasn't fair, it wasn't kind and it also with its dementedness then claimed my Mother.

Pearl who flew a plane and water-skied at 79. Pearl who's favorite hobby was to dance, fell and broke her hip and forgot how to walk. Pearl, who smiles and loves men and was so gracious, bit the nurse. Pearl, who still knows me, still lights up and converses in babble with extreme energy. Pearl with the great sense of humor is still trying a few quips. Pearl who yesterday told me she milked 40 cows is lost.

If it weren't for those who understand and support with ears and hearts and listening skills, I would walk in a fog thinking I was alone in this mist. The time has come for awareness for all of us. And we learn together. We learn of others on our journey. A fellow I met yesterday said that he believed that when the mind is filled with loss that it is already gone to God and that in that Eternal place. . .cows are getting milked, husbands and loved ones from the past are in sight and the music of the 20's and 30's is current. So who are we to say that someone is in the wrong. From that view. . .God is in his heaven and all is right with the world and with my Mom Pearl.

Reflections of Childhood In The Summerland

by Jeff Jasin

In the Summerland I know a place. A white cottage on a Silver Lake. In the cottage stayed an elderly couple. They were my grandparents and the keepers of this carefree haven which I visited on the vacations of my youth. Upon my arrival I was greeted with hugs and kisses accompanied by cries of happiness. They would say to me. "My, my look how much you've grown!" and 'It's so good to see you again." and "It seems like such a long time since the last time we saw you!" As I nuzzled the powdered cheeks of my grandmother and the wrinkled jowls of my grandfather, the scents of old lady's perfume and plain soap wafted into my nostrils and into the breeze that murmured and rustled in the tall pine trees. After a brief repast and content after a long journey the events preceding our arrival were recalled and reiterated and the whereabouts of old acquaintances recounted. Whereupon I would excuse myself from the table and scale the knotty pine stairs which echoed my drooping footsteps with a hollow resonance and fall into a small bed just my size with soft sheets dried on a clothesline in the open air and into a deep sleep.

I awakened to the clatter of the breakfast dishes and the rich aroma of fresh coffee. As I rubbed the sleep from my eyes I watched the shadows of the pine boughs playing on the wall above my bed. I dressed and scurried downstairs to the kitchen where I ate a hurried breakfast and then on outside through the screen door which announced my comings and goings with a creaking spring and a clamorous crash. In the morning the dew that sprinkled the sparse grass dampened the canvas of my sneakers as I wandered to and fro in search of a friend or as I endeavored to aid my grandfather with his chores in whatever manner a small child can be of assistance. When the chores were finished there was idle time for idyllic excursions. A walk in the woods, or a boat ride around the lake, or maybe even in the airplane. Where we would fly high above the ground and people looked like ants and houses like matchboxes, and the roads crisscrossed the fields and the woods as if the seams of a patchwork quilt.

Lunch was a summertime feast set on a tippy picnic table with a red and white checkered tablecloth. Hot dogs with ketchup, mustard, and relish. Tomatoes and potato chips, radishes, cucumbers, and pickles, with squeaky cheese curds and cold Wisconsin milk. Followed by a sweet watermelon with striped brown seeds and a yellow green rind. After lunch I gathered my beachtowel and pail and shovel and ventured down to the lake. There a bristle of flags and pennants flapped in the wind and the hot sun on the clear water reddened my fair and freckled skin. The high pitched laughter and squeals of glee resounded on the surface of the lake, like a calliope at an aquatic circus. Waterskiers in tow behind boats on bright tethers weaved up and down the shore with their skis slapping the waves like brisk applause. If the weather turned blustery I still had to be coaxed from the white capped waves to the foam flecked shore, blue lipped and purple veined to be bundled in a beachtowel and harried to the cottage. Where I exchanged my wet and sandy swimtrunks for trousers and a hooded sweatshirt. Though most of the time a copper sun falling from an enameled skies called the day to a close. I would retrieve my beachtowel and pail and shovel and trudge up the stairs to the cottage.

I donned a dapper ensemble for dinner. I held the hand of a loved one as we crossed the road to a dim, smoke filled establishment that had a stuffed moose with glass eyes and cobwebs in the antlers above the door. A good natured bartender named Wally served the patrons their refreshments and as I was famished from an afternoon of tireless exertion sometimes it seemed as if hours passed before dinner arrived. I gorged on fresh fish drenched in lemon juice and tartar sauce served with french fries and ketchup.

In the waning twilight of evening I climbed onto the lap of a loved one and embarked in an automobile to go to the fairgounds to see the fireworks. Perched on the bleachers and covered in blankets I waited impatiently in the gathering darkness for that which was to come. With a KABBOOOMMM. . . the fireworks began. Sputtering and sparking and arching high overhead before exploding into burning spiders and gigantic chrysanthemums. The townspeople and the weekenders accompanied the thunderous reports with OOOHH's and AAAHH's and sounds of delight. Fiery streamers and noisy screamers illumined the night with incendiaries and incandescent light. Then all too soon it had ended. After what seemed like a long walk to the automobile. It was back onto the beloved lap to see if we could see some of the deer who gather for the night not too far from here. So we drive slow so as not to miss or frighten them. " 'There they are!' 'Where?' 'There!' 'Shhhh!' " Their eyes glow bright green and their buff colored necks and heads are seen, in the tall grass, for a short while, before they're bound for the cover of nearby trees.

We are home and I am carried in the arms of a loved one up the knotty pine stairs and put into a small bed, just my size, with soft sheets dried on a clothesline in the open air, and I am already in a deep sleep.

JANIE JASIN

Creativity,"No Limits," Inc.

Janie Jasin is an inspiration-giver by profession. An enter-taining, dynamic, and sensitive speaker. Her presentations weave together humor, music, and audience participation, and have an extraordinary capacity to leave participants feeling refreshed, renewed, and just plain better.

PLANNING A MEETING?

Do you have a group that is interested in hearing Janie Jasin speak? She is available for seminars, workshops, and 30- to 45-minute breakfast, luncheon, or dinner talks.

Fees are based on the number of participants and the amount of time involved, plus travel expenses.

Please send more information on seminars:

Name of group: _____

Approximate number of people who will attend: _____

Meeting Date	**Location**
_____	_____

Send information to:

Name _____

Address _____

City _____ State _____ Zip _____

Home Phone: _____ Office Phone: _____

Janie Jasin, CSP
1743 Green Crest Dr.
Victoria, MN 55386
(952) 443-3086
Fax (952) 443-3081
www.janiespeaks.com